words at school

Printed and bound in the United Kingdom for the
Publishers Peter Haddock Ltd., Bridlington, England.
© Peter Haddock Ltd.

words at school

Colin Clark

Illustrated by Lesley McLaren

The boy is holding two balloons. If we **add** two balloons, then he has four. 2 **added** to 2 equals 4. 2+2=4.

We call all the letters that make words, from A to Z, the **alphabet**. The **alphabet** has 26 letters.

Do you want to know the time? **Ask** a policeman. **Ask** him to tell you.

What is the third letter of the alphabet?

An **atlas** is a book of maps. We use **atlases** at school to look at maps.

When the **bell** rings, it is time to go home. Teacher rings the **bell**.

Black is a colour. The words in this book are printed in **black**.

What kind of noise does your door bell make?

Blue is a colour. This girl is wearing a **blue** dress. Her shoes are also **blue**.

Brown is a colour. Here is a **brown** dog. The dog's kennel is also **brown**.

When we have a lot to do, we are **busy**. Bees always seem to be **busy**.

Have you had a busy day today?

Teacher writes in **chalk** on the board. Usually he uses white **chalk**. **Chalk** makes dust.

Our **class** is Primary II. We sit in a **class**room. Mrs Smith is our **class** teacher.

Playing with **clay** is great fun. It is messy. We make things out of **clay**.

Do you have chalk
and a blackboard at home?

A **clock** shows you what time it is. Alarm **clocks** wake us up in the morning.

A **compass** can show us which way to go. The **compass** needle always points to the north.

Computers at school help us to learn. We have a home **computer** for work and play.

Do you use a computer at school?

Teacher told us to **copy** the words. We must **copy** the words into our books.

Jack sits at a **desk** at school. Dad works at a **desk** in his office.

If we have 1 apple and 4 children, we must **divide** the apple into pieces.
This apple will **divide** into 8 pieces. How many will each child get?

Can you copy the words on this page?

If you **double** your money, you have twice as much as before. **Double** 5 is 10.

When you **draw** something, you make a **drawing**, or picture, of it with a pen or pencil.

I do not understand. Please **explain** it to me. Make it clear. Give me an **explanation**.

Do you like drawing and painting?
What do you like to draw?

Green is a colour. Grass is **green**. So are leaves. Dad's car is **green**.

Grey is a colour. Grandfather has lots of **grey** hair. Lots of winter days are **grey**.

Here is a **group** of children. Many people together are called a **group**.

Which is your favourite pop group?

A **gymnasium** or **gym** is a room at school where we do exercises to make our bodies healthy.

Cut the cake into two equal parts. We have **halved** it. We will have **half** each.

The whole school meets in the big **hall**. We have morning assembly in the **hall**.

Do you go to gym lessons?

This girl's **hobby** is collecting stamps. **Hobbies** are something to do to pass the time.

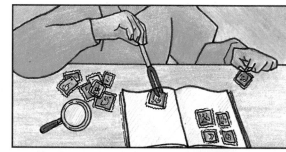

Your **initials** are the first letters of your names. **J**ohn **W**illiam **S**mith's **initials** are JWS.

We go to school to **learn** things. We find out about reading. We are **learning** to read.

What did you learn at school today?

We learn many **lessons** at school. Each **lesson** is something we must learn.

The alphabet has 26 **letters**. A is the first **letter** and Z is the last **letter**.

Something that we throw away is called **litter**. We must put it in the **litter** bin.

Do you always remember not to drop litter?

A **magnet** pulls iron towards it. We can pick up pins with a **magnet**.

A **map** is a drawing which shows countries, rivers, mountains, seas and cities. This is a **map** of Australia.

We **measure** how long, deep, wide or large something is. We also **measure** how much there is of something.

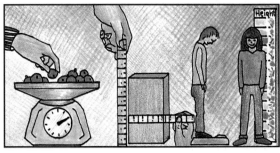

What do you use to measure how heavy you are?
Have you stood on scales?

Jack gave the wrong answer. He made a **mistake**, an error. He was **mistaken**.

The boy is making a **model** aircraft. A **model** is a small copy.

We learn to **multiply** at school. If we **multiply** 3 by 3, the answer is 9.

What is the answer if you multiply 3 by 4?
Is it 12?

A **name** is what someone or something is called. This boy is called Jack. His **name** is Jack.

The teacher has put a **notice** on the board. We must pay attention to the **notice**.

We count things or people in **numbers**. We **number** them. A **number** tells us how many there are.

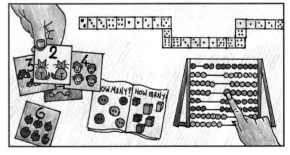

What is your lucky number?

Opposite means as different as possible. Cold is **opposite** to hot. Big and little are **opposites**. Up is **opposite** to down.

A **pattern** is the way in which colours and shapes are arranged. This dress has a pretty **pattern** on it.

A **quarter** is one of four equal parts. Fifteen minutes is a **quarter** of an hour. Two **quarters** are a half.

Is there a pattern on your bedroom wallpaper?

The teacher asks a **question** to find out if Laura knows the answer. He **questions** her.

The boys **queue** at the bus stop. They stand in a line. They form a **queue**.

I can **read** writing and printing. I **read** the words. I understand their meaning.

Can you read this question all by yourself?

Red is a colour. Ripe tomatoes are r**ed**. We colour things **red** to warn of danger.

Teacher keeps a **register**. A **register** is a list of the children in a class.

The boy has a **satchel** on his back. He carries his school things in his **satchel**.

What does your satchel look like? Is it red?

School is the place where we learn lessons. We learn to read and write at **school**.

Laura has a **set** of crayons, one of each colour. A **set** of things belong together.

Subtract means to take away from. **Subtract** one egg from six eggs and five eggs remain.

What else do you do at school?

We add things together to get the **sum**. The **sum** of 2 and 3 is 5.

The **teacher** is showing the boy how to read and write. He is **teaching** him.

We have a **test** at school to see how much we have learned. We are **tested**.

Do you have a nice teacher at school?

White is a colour. The paper in this book is **white**. Jack has a **white** shirt.

Andrew is **writing** his name. He uses a pen to **write** the letters that make the words.

Yellow is a colour. Butter is **yellow**, so are lemons. **Yellow** is a bright, happy colour.

How many yellow things can you see in the room?

These are the words you have learned in this book:

add	explain	notice
alphabet	green	number
ask	grey	opposite
atlas	group	pattern
bell	gymnasium	quarter
black	half	question
blue	hall	queue
brown	hobby	read
busy	initials	red
chalk	learn	register
class	lesson	satchel
clay	letter	school
clock	litter	set
compass	magnet	subtract
computer	map	sum
copy	measure	teacher
desk	mistake	test
divide	model	white
double	multiply	write
draw	name	yellow